French Prints in the Era of Impressionism and Symbolism

Colta Ives

The Metropolitan Museum of Art

Reprinted from *The Metropolitan Museum of Art Bulletin* (Summer 1988). Designed by Antony Drobinski, Emsworth Studios.

Photograph credits

Color photography by Malcolm Varon and black-and-white photography by The Metropolitan Museum of Art Photograph Studio unless otherwise noted: Albright-Knox Art Gallery, p. 32; Art Institute of Chicago, p. 6 (top); Art Resource, pp. 5 (bottom), 16; City of Manchester Art Galleries, p. 12; George Eastman House, p. 7; Fogg Art Museum, p. 8; Lynton Gardiner, p. 36; Metropolitan Museum Photograph Studio, pp. 6 (bottom), 32; Museum of Fine Arts, Boston, p. 48; National Gallery of Art, p. 28; Nelson-Atkins Museum of Art, p. 22; private collection, p. 10; State Museum Kröller-Müller, p. 47; courtesy of Mrs. John Hay Whitney, p. 54.

Cover: Edouard Vuillard. *The Game of Checkers.* From a suite of twelve lithographs published in 1899. Color lithograph, third state, 13¼ x 10½ in. (33.8 x 26.9 cm). Harris Brisbane Dick Fund, 1925 (25.70.15). **Inside front cover:** Paul Gauguin. *Design for a Plate—Leda*, 1889. Hand-colored zincograph, diam. 8 1/16 in. (20.5 cm). Rogers Fund, 1922 (22.82.2-1)

Director's Note

Visitors to the Museum's galleries for works of art on paper only occasionally encounter selections from our remarkable holdings of late nineteenth-century French prints. It is their fragility that limits their exhibition, not any lack of interest on our part, for exploration of the boxes in the print vaults is invariably rewarding. The publication of this *Bulletin* gives us a splendid opportunity to illustrate a number of these appealing images, which communicate the principles of Impressionism and Symbolism in the media of etching, woodcut, and lithography.

Those for whom the term "Impressionism" connotes canvases encrusted with colored pigments and enlivened with light may be intrigued to see here the graphic equivalents of these painterly aims, along with decisive evidence of the continued importance of drawing. It is almost always the masterful painter-draftsmen who are the printmakers of greatest interest to us—Dürer, Rembrandt, Goya, and Delacroix, and the artists represented on the following pages. Indeed, a theme of this publication is the congenial and informative relationship between an artist's paintings and his prints. We are fortunate to be able to demonstrate this consanguinity by pairing examples from our own collections; for instance, on pages 42 and 43, Vuillard's oil painting *Interior with Figure,* of 1896, with his color lithograph *Interior with a Hanging Lamp,* published in 1899.

Although many of our important Old Master prints were gifts or bequests of private collections, the nineteenth-century French prints have been acquired mainly by curatorial purchases, some made quite early in the Department's history. William M. Ivins, Jr., appointed first curator in 1916, acquired during the 1920s most of the lithographs by Degas, Manet, Gauguin, Bonnard, and Vuillard reproduced here.

During the late 1960s and early 70s, several significant purchases were made by Curator John J. McKendry to augment the small group of Degas's prints received from the bequest of Mr. and Mrs. H. O. Havemeyer in 1929. With the help of Douglas Dillon and funds from the Mr. and Mrs. Richard J. Bernhard Gift, nine prints were purchased, including the grand nocturnal monotype *The Fireside* (pp. 18-19), which will be shown in the major exhibition of Degas's work opening at the Museum in September.

During the last decade, under the curatorship of Colta Ives, the author of this text, our collections have experienced another burst of growth. Supplementing general purchase funds, gifts from Derald H. and Janet Ruttenberg, as well as the Scofield Thayer bequest have enriched the representation of works by Manet, Degas, Toulouse-Lautrec, and Pierre Bonnard, whose prints and book illustrations will be the subject of an exhibition to open at the Metropolitan late in 1989.

Philippe de Montebello
Director

Introduction

By the 1860s Paris had grown to a population of one and a half million citizens, whose appetite for entertaining and informative pictures was served by 1180 printing firms and a flourishing illustrated press. The picture-printing industry had only recently undergone its own revolution with the inventions of lithography and photography, the first entirely new techniques for multiplying images to be introduced since the practice of printing pictures from incised wood blocks and metal plates was developed in Europe during the fifteenth century.

The resulting expansion practically defies description. That over 1300 illustrated periodicals were launched between 1830 and 1900 suggests the scale of French production, as does the fact that by 1884 the color pictorial Sunday supplement to the *Petit journal* had reached an edition of one million.

It was as true in the nineteenth century as it was in the Renaissance, and as it is now, that a painter's reputation could be gained or lost in the press, and wise were the artists who realized, even as Dürer and Raphael did early on, that designs multiplied in print could spread their fame faster and farther than paintings. All of the artists represented in this *Bulletin* took up printmaking with the hope of increasing the visibility of their art. They saw their prints functioning as ambassadors-at-large, carrying to a wider audience evidence of their creativity. Thus, Paul Gauguin informed Vincent van Gogh late in January 1889 that he had "commenced a series of lithographs for publication in order to make myself known."

It may be said that artists draw to inform themselves, while they make prints to inform others. Prints, like paintings, require considerable preparation before their public presentation, and artists have often found it both resourceful and instructive to make prints for reproduction or reinterpretation of painted works. Manet's etched re-creation of his painting *Olympia* (opposite), the canvas that provoked outrage at the Salon of 1865, was conceived to illustrate Emile Zola's defense of the picture in a small publication occasioned by Manet's independent exhibition in May 1867. The narrow format of the pamphlet, however, forced Manet to compress his original composition into a tight, diminutive image that is more a memento than an accurate reproduction.

Manet was the most advanced artist of his day to reproduce his paintings in prints, upholding a tradition that was pronounced among the older masters he admired, particularly the painter-etcher Goya. A founding member of the Société des Aquafortistes, established in 1862 to foster creative interest in etching, Manet issued two portfolios of etched works, most of them based on his paintings, in 1862 and 1863. His periodic practice of the more modern medium of lithography, which he began about this time, intermittently stimulated other artists, eventually leading, in the last decade of the century, to the splendid outpouring of lithographs that are the subject of much of this publication.

Lithography was invented around 1796 in Germany by a Bavarian playwright, Alois Senefelder, who found he could duplicate his scripts cheaply by printing them from greasy crayons and inks applied to slabs of local limestone. Because the limestone retained designs applied to its surface through repeated printings, lithographs could be produced in almost unlimited quantities, offering extraordinary commercial possibilities.

It did not take long for lithography to find a broad range of applications in advertising, illustration, the popular press, and in the service of art; but by virtue of its practicality and diversified use, it was persistently plagued by crises of identity. Its glorious tenure during the 1820s and 30s in the hands of Goya, Géricault, and Delacroix was all too brief, and attempts in the 1860s to revive interest in the medium as a means for artists to duplicate their drawings failed. Etching was still the established artists' technique in the 1870s, when Fantin-Latour turned to lithography and persuaded Redon to exult in its tonal richness.

When Henri Fantin-Latour and Odilon Redon joined the Société des Artistes Lithographes Français, shortly after it was established in 1884, they found their fellow members were not painters but professional printers engaged in the manufacture of commercial reproductions of oil paintings. The practice of copying artworks in lithography, like the long tradition of reproductive engraving and etching that began in the sixteenth century, was soon to be entirely eclipsed, however, by photomechanical processes. From 1889 on, as lithography was relieved of its copying tasks, more and more artists began to adopt it as a means for creative expression.

By its very nature, printmaking was judged antithetical to the aims of most Impressionist painters, who believed that its technical procedures defeated spontaneity and failed to render the transient appearance of nature. Thus, it is not surprising that Monet, for instance, whose aim was to capture the evanescent effects of weather and light, made no prints at all. Edgar Degas and Camille Pissarro, however, who excelled as draftsmen and sought to preserve essential contours and forms in their art, each produced a body of work in etching and lithography that is distinctive, highly inventive, and entirely complementary to their paintings.

Degas, who owned a printing press and delighted in experimenting with new media, encouraged Pissarro by sending him proofs of his etchings with cheering messages. Degas's enchantment with the medium of monotype, probably inspired by the painterly etchings of Rembrandt, is further evidence of his long-term attachment to ink and the press, as is his often closely related work in lithography during the late 1870s and early 90s. "If Rembrandt had had lithography," he said, "God knows what wonder-

Edouard Manet, 1832–1883. *Olympia,* 1867. Etching, second state of six. Plate: 3⅜ × 8⅛ in. (8.8 × 20.1 cm). The Elisha Whittelsey Collection, The Elisha Whittelsey Fund, 1983 (1983.1093)

ful things he might have done with it."

By 1895, when France got the jump on Germany by organizing an exhibition honoring the centennial of lithography a year ahead of schedule, the renaissance of artistic lithography was well under way. Artists took advantage of technical and mechanical innovations (like the steam-powered press) that had advanced the commercial lithography industry since 1837, when Godefroy Engelmann and his son, Jean, patented the process they later called *chromolithographie.* The striking results of issuing prints in three to seven colors were publicly demonstrated by the poster artists of the era, who were largely responsible for the designation of the 1890s as the golden age of color lithography. The widespread popularity of the new colorful posters and artists' prints helped to inaugurate many of today's practices in print publishing, distribution, and private collecting.

By mid-decade readers of art journals like *La Plume* and *La Revue blanche* were offered prints as premiums, while subscribers to special limited editions of prints could obtain albums issued under the titles *L'Epreuve* (1894), *L'Estampe moderne* (1897), and *Germinal* (1899). Redon's *Auricular Cell* (p. 26), Gauguin's *Manao Tupapau* (p. 33), and Bonnard's *Family Scene* (p. 37) are all lithographs that first appeared in the highly successful collectors' series *L'Estampe originale,* published by André Marty between 1893 and 1895 and distributed in wrappers designed by artists, including Henri de Toulouse-Lautrec.

The most important publisher of limited-edition portfolios from 1896 to 1900 was Ambroise Vollard, who commissioned suites of color lithographs from the avant-garde painters who called themselves Nabis (after the Hebrew word for "messenger" or "prophet"). The medium of color lithography was remarkably sympathetic to the aims of these young painters, among them Pierre Bonnard, Edouard Vuillard, and Maurice Denis, who saw printmaking as a valuable ally in their campaign to break down old hierarchies of artistic expression and to bring art to a larger audience.

The Nabis had first directed their attentions toward the work of Gauguin,

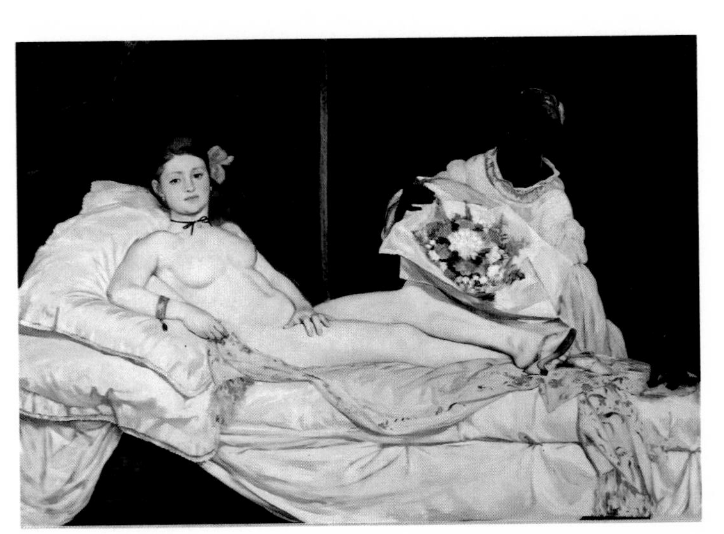

Edouard Manet. *Olympia,* 1863. Oil on canvas, 52⅜ × 74¾ in. (130.5 × 190 cm). Musée d'Orsay, Paris

whose strong colors and simplified forms represented scenes from everyday life not so much realistically as symbolically. Symbolism, which sought to evoke mood through suggestion rather than exact statement, became increasingly the dominant aesthetic, beginning with Redon in the 1880s and continuing to the end of the century.

The opposition between Impressionism's attachment to the fugitive appearances of the material world and Symbolism's probing evocations of the spiritual one was nowhere more potently expressed than in Gauguin's bold images. His revolutionary prints made from carved blocks of wood strike a primal chord—as he intended—transporting us to former times and exotic lands by their references to early sacred images and the woodcuts of Japan.

In their molding of an art style distinct from that of the Impressionists (even as their subject matter remained similar), the Nabis, and especially Bonnard and Vuillard (right, above), found fresh inspiration in the briskly rendered and luminously colorful ukiyo-e woodcuts (right, below), which became collectible in Paris after Western trade with Japan was resumed in 1856. Japanese artifacts began to appear as novel accessories in Impressionist paintings around 1868, when Manet showed a color woodcut by Kuniaki II as part of the decor in his portrait of Emile Zola. Soon the principles underlying this foreign art began to guide Parisian artists. The flattened forms, unusual perspectives, and insistent patterns used by Japanese printmakers enthralled particularly the younger generation of color lithographers and hastened still further artistic revolutions to come in the twentieth century. Toulouse-Lautrec, for whom the creation of color-lithographed actor portraits, playbill covers, and posters became a consuming activity, focused on the tart colors, dynamic lines, and animated figures in Kabuki theater prints by Sharaku and his contemporaries.

Certainly as significant as the influx of

Edouard Vuillard, 1868–1940. *The Tuileries,* 1895. Lithograph, 11 × 11⅛ in. (27.9 × 28.3 cm). The Art Institute of Chicago, Gift of the Print and Drawing Club (1953.191)

Hokusai Katsushika, 1760–1849. *Sazai Hall of the Temple of the 500 Rakan.* From *The Thirty-six Views of Fuji.* Color woodcut, 10¼ × 15¼ in. (26 × 38.7 cm). The Henry L. Phillips Collection, Bequest of Henry L. Phillips, 1939 (JP 2984)

Louis-Jean Delton, before 1820–after 1896. *Woman on Horseback, Taking a Jump,* 1884. Black-and-white photograph. International Museum of Photography at George Eastman House, Rochester, New York

Japanese woodcuts, though perhaps less easily identifiable, was the impact of the invention of photography in 1839. Photography's unrivaled achievement in verisimilitude now forced painters and printmakers to identify their art in other terms. The polished precision of photographs emphasized by contrast the aberrant qualities of handmade pictures, and beginning with Impressionism, artists believed they should make the most of the differences. "I consider impressionism an altogether new departure which inevitably diverges from anything that is mechanical, such as photography, etc. ... Thus I shall get away as much as possible from anything that gives the illusion of an object ... ," wrote Gauguin in 1888, justifying his purposeful distortions and seemingly arbitrary use of colors.

At the same time that photography rushed painters toward abstraction and away from realism, it also forced their reevaluation of the technical and mental processes of picture-making, leading them to question the structure of pictorial space and helping them to define the dynamics special to the hand-designed image. The photographer's usurpation of the window on the world, which had belonged to the painter since the Renaissance, thus presented new liberties and eye-opening opportunities.

Manet used photographs mechanically, as scaled-down copies of his paintings that he traced to prepare etchings and lithographs. Degas, Bonnard, and Vuillard, on the other hand, involved themselves in photography's own aesthetic, taking snapshots of family and friends in broad daylight and by the murky light of oil lamps, occasionally developing film themselves, as Vuillard did in a soup plate. French artists now had at hand a wealth of photographic images that had been accumulating in Parisian sitting rooms since around 1860: carte-de-visite portraits, stereograph cityscapes, family pictures, and travel views in elaborately bound albums. By this time also, photography's fast exposures had demonstrated the strange distortions of stopped action, as it offered a fresh, casual outlook. The Nabis lithographers Bonnard and Vuillard, whose aim was to draw us directly into the panorama of Paris life, were especially attracted to the candid organization of many photographs, and they adopted without hesitation one of the favorite focal points of the camera, the foreground, where the field of activity unites with the picture's surface. The position of the picture's participants and of its observers now came very close to being the same, and as earlier established barriers seemed to dissolve, the question Does art follow life, or is it the other way around? presented itself for debate.

Edouard Manet. *Racecourse at Longchamp,* 1864. Gouache, 9⁹⁄₁₆ × 22⁷⁄₈ in. (23 × 58 cm). Fogg Art Museum, Harvard University, Cambridge, Massachusetts

In 1857, only two decades after horse racing had been introduced in France by Anglophiles, a large track and viewing stands were inaugurated at Longchamp in the Bois de Boulogne. The races there soon attracted thousands of Parisians, among them Edouard Manet and Edgar Degas, both of whom began painting the racetrack early in the 1860s.

The subject of horse racing was a relatively novel one for French artists, and there are few precedents to prepare us for Manet's explosive vision of the Longchamp track (opposite). Sporting prints were popular at the time among the British, but only the large aquatints after paintings by Francis Calcraft Turner (ca. 1782–1846), like his *Leamington Grand Steeple Chase* (1837), begin to approach the dynamic effect of Manet's piece, which boldly places the spectator in the path of the oncoming horses. In its openness and linear vitality this work surpasses even Goya's grand bullfight lithographs, Géricault's muscular horse prints, and Daumier's energetic satires.

Manet's lithograph has long been a puzzle, on account of both its unfinished appearance and the difficulties in securing its date. The print derives from an oil painting that Manet planned to exhibit in 1865 and later cut into pieces—which is survived by a gouache drawing (above) presumed to be a study for that panoramic canvas. When Manet re-created this subject as a lithograph, the fuller (squarer) format of the standard-size printing stone evidently induced him to expand the initial long and narrow composition.

Challenged not only to enlarge the sky but also to invent a new foreground, Manet hastily filled in a throng of spectators and carriages along the extended track. His scribbles at the far right, which now appear so expressive and modern, probably attest to the fact that this print represents work still in progress. Few, if any, impressions of the lithograph were printed during Manet's lifetime; his widow initiated the publication of the first edition in 1884.

Three other surviving pictures chart the history of this composition, which engaged Manet's attention for nearly a decade. They include a painting (now in the Art Institute of Chicago) believed to date about 1867 that focuses on only one-fifth of the print's field of vision and, like a camera's zoom lens, pulls us close to the action. Two later works from the period 1872–75 (a drawing in the Louvre and a small oil at the National Gallery in Washington) concentrate still more intently on the cluster of horses and the dust cloud at their feet.

Edouard Manet. *The Races,* ca. 1865. Lithograph on china paper, 1884 edition. Image: 15¼ × 20⅛ in. (38.7 × 51.1 cm). Rogers Fund, 1920 (20.17.2)

Edouard Manet. *Berthe Morisot with a Bunch of Violets,* 1872. Oil on canvas, 21¾ × 15 in. (55 × 38 cm). Private Collection

Edouard Manet. *Portrait of Berthe Morisot,* 1872–74. Lithograph, 8 × 5½ in. (20.5 × 14.2 cm). Harris Brisbane Dick Fund, 1923 (23.21.22)

The most memorable face in the works of Manet is surely that of Berthe Morisot (1841–1895), a painter herself whose talent was sparked by close contact with her portraitist. Morisot was copying a Rubens in the Louvre when she was introduced to Manet by Henri Fantin-Latour in 1867. After that, she and her sister Edma, also an aspiring artist, spent many congenial evenings in the company of the Manet family.

Morisot is featured in several of Manet's paintings, beginning in about 1868–69 with her appearance as the magnetic but distracted *maja* in *The Balcony* and ending in 1874, a year marked by the death of her father, her participation in the first Impressionist exhibition, and her marriage to Manet's brother, Eugène. Manet variously portrayed Morisot as a fashionable beauty, a haggard mourner, and, in his 1872 oil (left), as a bright-eyed French version of Eliza Doolittle, caught in appealing disarray. He produced an etching and two lithographs related to the 1872 painting. The etching conveys an anxious mood in its wiry lines, shaded countenance, and off-center pose, while the lithographs seem to neglect their subject somewhat nonchalantly in order to pursue an independent course of balancing black and white, line and mass.

The lithograph shown here (opposite) follows the essential contours of Manet's painting so carefully that we assume the artist traced a photograph of his canvas in order to transfer its composition to the printing stone. There is a bracing, decidedly graphic quality in the printed portrait's lack of descriptive modeling or mid-tones. The vigor of its soft, oily drawing anticipates Manet's abundant production near the end of his career of pastel half- or bust-length portraits, which a friend, the art critic Théodore Duret, explained as "a diversion" that "gained him the company of the engaging women who came to pose for him."

Henri Fantin-Latour, 1836–1904. *Bouquet of Roses*, 1879. Oil on canvas, 17 × 15 in. (43.9 × 38 cm). City of Manchester Art Galleries, Manchester, England

Although he attained fame for his pictures of flowers, Fantin-Latour was by no means an open-air painter. He customarily collected his subjects from the garden and brought them indoors to arrange before his canvas. In the undisturbed stillness of the studio, the artist could study each bloom with the same reverent attention he devoted to the individuals who sat for his precisely rendered portraits.

In the summer of 1879, when Fantin painted the *Bouquet of Roses* (left), he enthusiastically wrote to a friend, the artist Otto Scholderer, "This year I find the flowers more beautiful than ever." His special satisfaction with this painting is evidenced by his faithful reproduction of the canvas in a black-and-white lithograph of the same proportions (opposite). Fantin apparently traced his oil painting on treated paper in order to transfer the picture onto the printing stone and then proceeded to handle the lithographic crayon in a lavish yet delicately restrained way, surely following the example of Delacroix, who could coax a sense of color from even the monochromatic.

Fantin exhibited this lithograph, the only still life among his nearly two hundred otherwise figural prints, at the Paris Salon of 1880. It was also shown that year at the Dudley Gallery in London, where Fantin's flower pieces found their most consistently supportive audience. Rose breeders in Victorian England were by this time in keen competition with the French, who had dominated the field since Empress Josephine's creation of vast rose beds at Malmaison. There was a surge in the development of hybrids and new strains, among them a pink variety of the full and fragrant Centifolia group that was named in Fantin's honor.

Henri Fantin-Latour. *Bouquet of Roses,* 1879. Transfer lithograph, 16⅜ × 14⅛ in. (41.6 × 35.9 cm). Anonymous Gift, 1985 (1985.1047)

Edgar Degas, 1834–1917. *Mademoiselle Marie Dihau,* 1868. Oil on canvas, 8¾ × 10¾ in. (22.2 × 27.3 cm). Bequest of Mrs. H. O. Havemeyer, 1929, H. O. Havemeyer Collection (29.100.182)

Degas was tireless in his pursuit of every possible artistic experiment and innovation. He explored new subject matter, adopted unusual angles of vision, and worked with techniques that had scarcely ever been used. Between 1876 and about 1893 he produced approximately five hundred monotypes, each a unique image created from an oily ink drawing he put through the press. Some of these monotypes were transferred to lithographic stones to be printed in larger editions; a great many laid the groundwork for finished pastels.

Degas made only fifteen or so monotypes that are as small as *The Jet Earring* (right), and practically all of them are informal portrait studies as quirky as Rembrandt's little etchings of heads. In this densely worked miniature, on the scale of the calling-card-sized photographs that were popular at the time, the treatment of the subject is suggestive more of still life than of portraiture. Purposefully directing the woman's face away from the viewer in the "lost profile" commonly featured in 1870s fashion plates, Degas focused instead on her millinery, coiffure, and jewelry.

Degas was remarkably alert to the accessories of modern women's dress, as his oils and pastels of ladies' hat shops done between 1882 and 1886 vividly attest. In these and in an earlier canvas (opposite) juxtaposing Marie Dihau's profile and her carpeted travel bag, fashionable effects are very richly rendered. Mlle Dihau, like her brother Désiré, a bassoonist whom Degas also painted, was a talented instrumentalist, as well as a singer. Degas later portrayed her playing the piano, but in this small canvas he showed her seated in a Parisian restaurant, prepared for the return home to Lille.

Edgar Degas. *The Jet Earring,* ca. 1877–80. Monotype, 3³⁄₁₆ × 2¾ in. (8.2 × 7 cm). Anonymous Gift, in memory of Francis Henry Taylor, 1959 (59.651)

Edgar Degas. *Aux Ambassadeurs*, 1877. Pastel over monotype, 14 9/16 × 10 5/8 in. (37 × 27 cm). Musée des Beaux-Arts, Lyons

The art of Degas amazes us again and again with its ingenuity. It records what was once relatively commonplace, but interprets the everyday in a pictorial language arresting for its unexpected accents and intonations. Degas, in mid-career, was attracted to the study of entertainers—especially dancers and singers—whom he watched in performance and in backstage preparations. He attended the Opéra and also the open-air cafés of the Champs-Elysées, where he could watch the spectacle of a *chanteuse* tossing raucous songs into the summer night.

These two pictures of Emélie Bécat at the Café des Ambassadeurs, singing amid the dazzle of gas lamps, fireworks, and moonlight, are among at least forty-five monotypes, lithographs, and etchings produced between 1876 and 1879 that reflect Degas's fascination with a popular French diversion, the café concert. His view over a tangle of heads and instruments conveys the press of the crowd and evokes the clamorous mix of voices, stringed melodies, and exploding rockets. The special excitement of Paris at night is expressed by the singer's broad gesture and by the chandelier shining into the darkness.

To represent night scenes like these, Degas almost always began with a plate totally blackened with ink, from which light-struck forms were then extracted. He sometimes transferred the image onto a polished stone, so that its dramatic contrasts could be retained and printed repeatedly by lithography (right); in an alternative technique, he embedded a unique impression of the inked plate in layers of colored pastels (left).

Edgar Degas. *Mlle Bécat at the Café des Ambassadeurs,* 1877–78. Lithograph. Image: 8⅛ × 7⅝ in. (20.6 × 19.4 cm). Rogers Fund, 1919 (19.29.3)

Edgar Degas. *The Fireside,* ca. 1876–77.
Monotype, 16⁵⁄₁₆ × 23⅛ in. (41.5 × 58.6 cm).
Purchase, Harris Brisbane Dick Fund, The Elisha Whittelsey Collection, The Elisha Whittelsey Fund and C. Douglas Dillon Gift, 1968 (68.670)

Degas's enduring fascination with the human figure led him to venture beyond the panorama of Parisian public life to enter the city's innermost private domains. As he strove to represent the female body with greater truth, women engaged in the intimate rituals of both the bath and the brothel became regular themes. "The nude has always been portrayed in postures that presuppose an audience, but my women are simple, straightforward women, concerned with nothing beyond their physical existence . . . ," Degas reportedly explained to the English writer George Moore in 1886. "It's as though one were peeping through a keyhole."

During the 1870s, when novels by Huysmans, Edmond de Goncourt, and Zola focused on the flourishing profession of prostitution, Degas also studied the world of the *maisons closes,* producing about fifty monotypes that depict the women's routines. Most of these smudged-ink prints are rather comic grotesques, like peep-show illustrations to a bawdy story, but unlike the later, crude romps that Picasso designed—which Degas's scenes did much to inspire—they seem to have been intended for a limited audience.

Very rarely did Degas treat a brothel scene on the monumental scale and seriousness of *The Fireside,* which is one of the largest of all his monotypes and perhaps the most evocative. It is a somber and secretive work, made so by the artist's selective wiping of the blackened plate with a cloth, a brush, and his own fingers in order to let the forms in the dark room emerge as if illuminated by firelight. The ponderous figures, solidly built but faceless, are mysterious and troubling, imparting something of the despairing gloom of Greek tragedy.

Edgar Degas. *After the Bath III,* 1891–92. Lithograph, first state of two. Image: 9¾ × 9 in. (24.4 × 22.3 cm). Bequest of Clifford A. Furst and Harris Brisbane Dick Fund, by exchange, 1972 (1972.571)

Edgar Degas. *After the Bath III,* 1891–92. Lithograph, second (final) state. Image: 9⅝ × 9 in. (24.7 × 22.8 cm). The Elisha Whittelsey Collection, The Elisha Whittelsey Fund, 1987 (1987. 1091)

It was the human figure in all its variety of movement that attracted Degas early in life; later he preferred the more concentrated and extended study of a single pose. Several oil paintings and pastels, a large number of drawings, and a series of six lithographs made between 1891 and 1892 chart Degas's exploration of one compelling theme, that of the standing long-haired woman who bends sideways either to wash or to dry herself after a bath.

Degas's interest in monumental depictions of the female bather can be traced back to his youth, when he took the trouble to persuade a school friend's father, M. Valpinçon, to change his mind and lend Ingres's great *Bather* to the Exposition Universelle of 1855. It was not until the late 1870s that Degas himself started to portray nude bathers, a theme that he would continue to explore for some thirty years. He roundly rejected the usual practice of employing goddesses, odalisques, or other legendary figures as pretexts for artistic renderings of the nude. "Two centuries ago," he declared, "I would have painted Susannah at the bath. Today, I paint only women in their tubs."

As completely contemporary and unpretentiously down-to-earth as Degas's models were, he could not always prevent himself from transforming them into figures of a sculptural grace that recalls classical ideas of perfection. In lithographs evolved from a single image (left and opposite), Degas progressively refined and refocused his vision so that physical reality seemed to dissolve, as if the boudoir had been elevated to Mount Olympus. Perhaps it is Degas's transformation of the ordinary into the ideal that makes his art so intriguing.

Edgar Degas. *After the Bath* (large version), 1891–92. Lithograph, fifth (final) state. Image: 11⅞ × 12¼ in. (30.2 × 31.5 cm). Bequest of Clifford A. Furst, by exchange, 1974 (1974.547.1)

Camille Pissarro, 1830–1903. *Wooded Landscape at L'Hermitage, Pontoise,* 1879. Oil on canvas, 18⁵⁄₁₆ × 22¹⁄₁₆ in. (46.5 × 56 cm). The Nelson-Atkins Museum of Art, Kansas City, Missouri. Gift of Dr. and Mrs. Nicholas C. Packard

Of all the Impressionist painters, Camille Pissarro was the most consistently devoted to printmaking. He began with rather perfunctory line etchings in 1863, but not until after his meeting with Degas in 1878 did his truly remarkable work commence. It was the proselytizing Degas who no doubt encouraged Pissarro to explore a greater variety of printmaking techniques and to experiment with such unconventional tools as metal brushes and sandpaper.

Degas's project to found a journal illustrated with artists' prints prompted Pissarro to manufacture an especially well-resolved and finished work, the *Wooded Landscape at L'Hermitage, Pontoise* (opposite). A complex combination of soft-ground etching, aquatint, and drypoint, the print reproduces in a surprisingly effective manner both the tremulous surface and the bracing configurations of his oil painting of the same year (right). (At this particular stage of his career, Pissarro was painting canvases that seemed scarcely able to contain all the terrain he compressed into them.)

Although the image was reversed in printing, the etching's composition is in nearly all respects faithful to that of the painting. Its vigorous texture of monochromatic tones and accents compensates for the absence of color. Reinforced in the graphic interpretation is the principal element of the picture: the pierced veil of trees, which tantalizes us with a partial vision of the terrain beyond, rather as an elaborate iron screen in a medieval cathedral dramatically prepares visitors for their arrival.

Pissarro must have felt a sting of disappointment when *Le Jour et la nuit,* Degas's magazine for which the print was intended, failed to materialize. At the Impressionist exhibition of 1880 he took the opportunity to display his tour de force by mounting together four states of the etching to demonstrate its technically elaborate development.

Camille Pissarro. *Wooded Landscape at L'Hermitage, Pontoise,* 1879. Soft-ground etching, aquatint and drypoint; sixth (final) state, 8¾ × 10⅝ in. (21.8 × 26.8 cm). Rogers Fund, 1921 (21.46.1)

Odilon Redon, 1840–1916. *L'Armure,* 1891. Charcoal and conté crayon, 20 × 14¼ in. (50.7 × 36.8 cm). Harris Brisbane Dick Fund, 1948 (48.10.1)

Entering the art of Odilon Redon, we escape the constraints of the physical world to gaze upon the dazzling terrain of the imagination. As a shy and lonely boy in his uncle's remote, old house, Redon discovered that books, pictures, and music opened windows onto marvelous vistas. From that time on, throughout his long life, he maintained a childlike attachment to the world of fantasy and dreams.

Young Redon was initiated into the rites of printmaking, particularly etching, at Rodolphe Bresdin's studio in Bordeaux, which looked out on the cemetery where Goya lay. Before long, however, he broke from the fussy practices of his eccentric master to find new freedom in the medium of charcoal. When, a decade or so later, Fantin-Latour suggested that he multiply his drawings by means of lithography, Redon's practice of printmaking was vigorously renewed, and between 1879 and 1908 he produced close to two hundred lithographs.

Redon called his works drawn in charcoal (left) and those printed in lithographic ink (opposite) "noirs," for both their essential substance and resonance were black. "One must respect black," he wrote. "Nothing prostitutes it. It does not please the eye and it awakens no sensuality. It is the agent of the mind far more than the most beautiful color of the palette or the prism."

For Redon, the distinction between mind and matter was blurred. Working before Freud's publication of the *Interpretation of Dreams* in 1899, he was virtually the only graphic artist to explore territory inaccessible to human sight, declaring it his mission to "put the logic of the visible at the service of the invisible." It was to the memory of his friend Armand Clavaud, the botanist who opened his eyes to the living universe seen through a microscope's lens, that he dedicated his suite of six lithographs entitled *Songes (Daydreams),* which includes the dark room's window looking out to daylight.

Odilon Redon. *Le Jour (Daylight),* 1891. From the series *Songes (Daydreams).* Lithograph, 8¼ × 6⅐₃₂ in. (21 × 15.6 cm). Rogers Fund, 1920 (20.30.6)

Odilon Redon. *Auricular Cell,* 1893. Lithograph, 10½ × 9¹³⁄₁₆ in. (26.7 × 24.9 cm). Rogers Fund, 1922 (22.82.1–18)

Redon's *Auricular Cell* (left) reflects his attraction to the works of Eugène Delacroix, the Romantic painter who had been the first to use lithography as a means of vivid personal expression. The medallionlike format of the image contains a face reminiscent of villainous characters in Delacroix's prints, especially Mephistopheles, the Prince of Darkness, to whom he gave spectacular form in his illustrations to *Faust* (1825).

Literature motivated much of Delacroix's art, as it did Redon's; but while Delacroix was drawn to the tragedies of Goethe and Shakespeare, Redon a generation later turned to the works of Baudelaire, Flaubert, and Poe. He was keenly sympathetic to the Symbolist poets, who insisted, as he did, upon the importance of the mysterious and the obscure.

In these two lithographs Redon celebrates the sensual power of hearing. Both prints show avid listeners: in an alert, satanic profile and a serene, bemused one. *The Celestial Art* (opposite) is devoted to the appreciation of music shared by Redon and the Symbolists. As Mallarmé theorized that good poetry should be "allusive music," Redon, an accomplished violinist, aspired to an art capable of evoking associations and feelings the way that music does. The themes of Berlioz and Beethoven enraptured him, and in 1893 a performance of Debussy's "La Demoiselle élue" moved him to send the composer one of his works. "My drawings inspire and do not define themselves," Redon explained. "They place us just as music does in the ambiguous world of the indeterminate."

Redon's depiction of an entranced music lover, drifting in the landscape of the mind, dates to 1894, the year of his first important one-man exhibition. Unfortunately, he received little acclaim, and although he soon abandoned black and white for color, he still failed to attract a following. Not until the generation of the Surrealists did he begin to receive his due.

Odilon Redon. *The Celestial Art,* 1894.
Lithograph, 12⅜ × 10⅛ in. (31.6 × 25.7 cm).
Gift of A. W. Bahr, 1958 (58.547.26)

Paul Gauguin, 1848–1903. *Breton Girls Dancing, Pont-Aven,* 1888. Oil on canvas, 28⅛ × 36½ in. (71.4 × 92.8 cm). National Gallery of Art, Washington, D.C.

After the financial crash of 1882, Paul Gauguin, who had been a stockbroker until then, decided to devote himself to painting full-time. Determined to flee the cursed "European craze for money," and a voyager since his youth, he set out to find the elusive unspoiled terrain, the ideal community, the Garden of Eden that could nourish his spirit and his art.

In 1886 Gauguin moved to the Breton village of Pont-Aven, where a colony of artists had settled to paint the picturesque peasants, the slate-roofed houses, and the Gothic steeples huddled in the valley of the Aven River. Not only was this outpost quieter and cheaper than Paris, but the simple rusticity of its landscape and people presented a cure to the world-weary artist. "I love Brittany," Gauguin wrote to his friend Emile Schuffenecker. "I find wildness and primitiveness there. When my wooden shoes ring on this granite, I hear the muffled, dull, and powerful tone which I try to achieve in painting."

In June 1888 Gauguin began painting a scene of three Breton girls dancing a *ronde* in the hayfields of Pont-Aven (above). The canvas was exhibited in Paris at Boussod and Valadon in November of that year and was to have been sold by the art dealer Theo van Gogh. The buyer, however, required that Gauguin change the picture slightly by altering the form of the hand of the dancer closest to the edge of the frame. Gauguin accomplished this during his stay with Vincent van Gogh in Arles that summer, but his picture was not sold until autumn. By that time Gauguin had already reinterpreted his painting in a suite of ten prints that are souvenirs of his work in Martinique, Brittany, and Arles. The album afforded Gauguin the opportunity to simplify, and to further distill into near-abstraction, compositions that he now outlined in black tusche (lithographic ink) and printed on sunny, mustard-colored paper (opposite).

In this print the Breton girl with the troublesome hand has been deleted from the summer haying dance, along with much of the surrounding landscape. By eliminating some of the elements in his earlier painting and exaggerating others, the artist diminished his picture's scenic value but intensified its emotional content. Often mindful of the uneasy side to the naïve spirit, Gauguin repeatedly alluded to the anxiety underlying seemingly ideal but isolated communities.

Paul Gauguin. *The Pleasures of Brittany,* 1889. Zincograph on yellow paper. Image: 7 15/16 × 9 1/2 in. (20.2 × 24.1 cm). Rogers Fund, 1922 (22.82.2–11)

Paul Gauguin. *Ia Orana Maria (Ave Maria)*, 1891.
Oil on canvas, 44¾ × 34½ in. (113.6 × 87.6 cm).
Bequest of Sam A. Lewisohn, 1951 (51.112.2)

Gauguin's hard-won sojourn in Tahiti from 1891 to 1893 resulted in over sixty fine paintings. Among them is a Maori-Christian Adoration (left) the painter produced in the first months after his arrival, in which he celebrated the unspoiled luxuriance of the tropical world. Gauguin later recalled the allure of his newfound home: "It really is open-air life, although intimate, in the thickets and the shaded brooks, those whispering women in an immense palace decorated by Nature itself with the riches which Tahiti holds. Hence these fabulous colours and this fiery but softened and silent air."

After returning to Paris sick and exhausted, Gauguin reminisced rather poetically about his South Seas life in a highly romanticized journal, *Noa Noa*. To illustrate these memoirs, he undertook the production of ten woodcuts, which, like his zincographs of some five years before, re-created the principal motifs of his paintings in bold graphic terms. On this occasion Gauguin incised symbolic figures in wood blocks, which he inked and printed by hand with obvious love of the craft. Although the blocks he cut were the standard type used in commercial wood-engraved illustration, Gauguin's techniques were wholly unorthodox and purposely crude. Gouge, chisel, knife, needle, and sandpaper were his tools now, just as they had been in Brittany when he carved wooden reliefs that had the appearance of primitive artifacts.

Gauguin's Polynesian Eve, who in the woodcut opposite plucks tropical fruit under the watchful eye of a serpent, figures in several works executed over a period of a decade, beginning with a remembrance of Martinique painted in 1890 and culminating in a striking canvas dated 1892. This earth goddess's statuesque posture, like that of the Holy Mother's attendants in his Adoration, derives from the sacred sculptures of Borobudur. Gauguin studied the Javanese temple reliefs in photographs that he probably obtained at the Paris Exposition Universelle of 1889.

Paul Gauguin. *Nave Nave Fenua (Delightful Land),* 1893–94. Color woodcut, 13⅞ × 8 in. (35.2 × 20.3 cm). Harris Brisbane Dick Fund, 1936 (36.6.4)

Paul Gauguin. *Manao Tupapau,* 1892. Oil on burlap, mounted on canvas, 28½ × 36⅜ in. (72.3 x 92.3 cm). Albright-Knox Art Gallery, Buffalo, New York, A. Conger Goodyear Collection

Opposite
Paul Gauguin. *Manao Tupapau (Watched by the Spirits of the Dead),* 1894. Lithograph, 7⅛ × 10⅝ in. (18 × 27.1 cm). Rogers Fund, 1922 (22.82.1–53)

In his largely fictional but nonetheless compelling diary, *Noa Noa,* Gauguin tells how he came home late one night to find his young native wife frozen in terror before a ghostly apparition engendered by sparkling phosphorescences: "Tehura lay motionless, naked, belly down on the bed: she stared up at me, her eyes wide with fear, and she seemed not to know who I was. . . . I had never seen her beauty so moving. . . . Perhaps she took me, with my anguished face, for one of those legendary demons or specters, the *Tupapaus* that filled the sleepless nights of her people."

Numerous paintings and prints came to be inspired by this dramatic episode, in which Gauguin's own domestic life fell under the spell of the supernatural. The motif of the reclining female figure was not, however, a new one for Gauguin, having entered his art as early as 1881, when his sleeping daughter Aline became the model for an oil study, *The Little Dreamer.* A decade later, the theme of the outstretched nude took on a new meaning for Gauguin when he painted a copy of Manet's *Olympia* (see page 5). Manet's Parisian courtesan was served by a maid, but when Gauguin depicted his own *vahine* the following year (above), he showed her attended by natives, or perhaps idols carved from the trunks of coco palms. What is most striking about this Polynesian nude is her unexpected, rigid posture, expressing fright rather than feminine allure.

For evidence of Gauguin's daring and versatility one need not look far beyond the three works illustrated here, where a single painted theme is elaborated in one print and simplified in another, according to properties inherent in the chosen medium. Gauguin details the flowery exoticism of his tale in sinuous ink drawing and tints on polished stone (opposite, above) but summons up its dark strains with heavy pigments and boldly gouged wood (opposite, below).

Paul Gauguin. *Te Po (Eternal Night),* 1893–94. Color woodcut, 8 × 14 in. (20.4 × 35.6 cm). Harris Brisbane Dick Fund, 1936 (36.6.12)

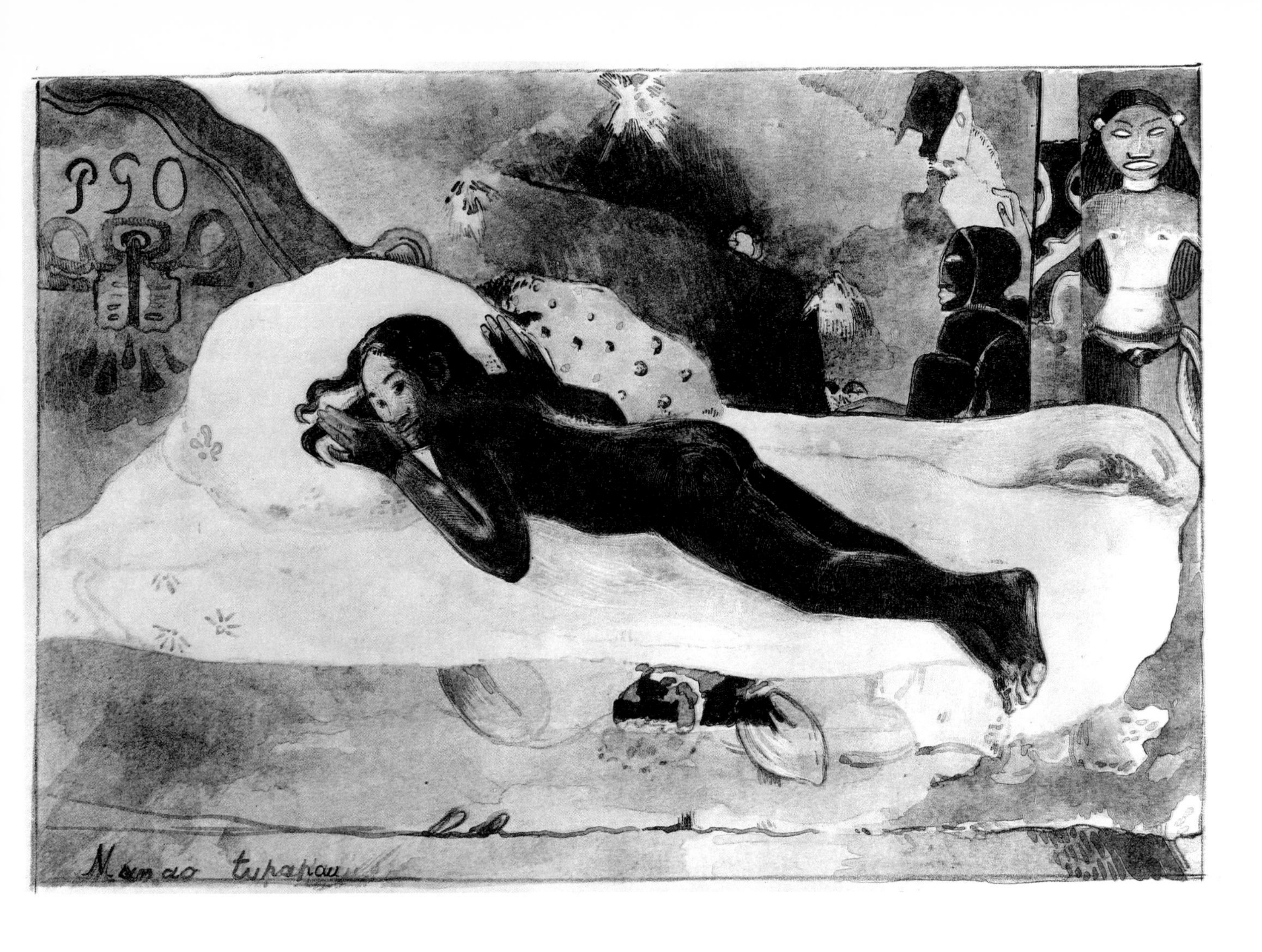
Manao tupapau

Maurice Denis, 1870–1943. *Amour,* ca. 1899. Cover for a suite of twelve lithographs. Color lithograph, 21 × 16¼ in. (54 × 43 cm). Harris Brisbane Dick Fund, 1941 (41.19.3[1])

Maurice Denis. *Les Attitudes sont faciles et chastes,* ca. 1899. From the suite *Amour.* Color lithograph, 15⅛ × 11 in. (38.5 × 28 cm). Harris Brisbane Dick Fund, 1941 (41.19.3 [4])

Maurice Denis's theories on art are often quoted because the pronouncements he made at the end of the last century seem to justify the art revolutions in ours. Actually, Gauguin's principles of art, transmitted to Denis by the painter Paul Sérusier, were the basis for Denis's famous directive of 1890: "It must be remembered that any painting—before being a war horse, a nude woman, or some anecdote—is essentially a flat surface covered with colors arranged in a certain order." This declaration of the precedence of material substance over subject matter seems to give the blessing not only to Neo-Impressionists and Nabis but also to Fauves, Cubists, and Abstract Expressionists.

However forward-looking Denis may seem in his writing, he nonetheless reveals in his art a deep and abiding attraction to the past. Like the Pre-Raphaelite painters in England, he found inspiration in quattrocento painting, which he studied in Italy during 1895. Denis, who considered his true mission the revitalization of Christian art, took great interest in the religious frescoes of Florence and Rome, and in early prayer sheets and manuscripts. A devout Catholic, he eventually became the major religious painter of his time.

Denis's profound belief in the spiritual and his outright antagonism toward realism made him a particularly sympathetic spokesman for the painters of the Symbolist generation. Like them, he was strongly influenced by Gauguin's early mystical works painted in Brittany (some of which Denis owned), in which sinuous lines weave together abstract pictorial elements.

In a suite of twelve lithographs completed around 1899, Denis displayed the distinctive lyrical style that he developed in his youth and remained faithful to throughout his career. His portfolio *Amour* was inspired by passages in his diary written at the time of his betrothal, when sentiment inspired turtledoves, moonlight, roses, and chestnut blossoms.

Les attitudes sont faciles et chastes

Pierre Bonnard, 1867–1947. *Mother and Child (Mme Claude Terrasse and Her Son Charles),* 1893. Oil on canvas, 15½ × 11¾ in. (37 × 30 cm). Collection of Alice Mason, New York

Young Pierre Bonnard's first commercial success, a design to advertise France-brand champagne, was executed in color lithography, a medium he was to find both sympathetic and instructive. "I've discovered a lot that applies to painting by doing color lithography," he later noted. "When you have to judge tonal relationships by juggling with four or five colors, superimposing them or juxtaposing them, you learn a great deal." Color lithography disciplined Bonnard in the elimination of all but the essentials in his art and also encouraged him to experiment with the flattened abstraction that so charmed him in color woodcuts by the Japanese. Thus, when translating a family portrait from the medium of painting (right) to that of printmaking (opposite), he isolated and exaggerated the scene's most decorative elements: its serpentine outlines and insistent patterns.

Like ukiyo-e artists he admired, Bonnard sought to recapture the small moments of warmth or whimsy that had enlivened his day. The incidents were generally refined by his memory into a few simple specifics he then rearranged as one might blooms in a bouquet. In the end, his picture might be more faithful to the spirit of an occasion than to its circumstances, for the impetus to evoke an episode rather than to describe it was strongly felt by Symbolist artists.

In the early years of his career Bonnard painted many idyllic scenes drawn from his family's enjoyment of the gardens surrounding their house at Grand-Lemps. Often, he adopted a bird's-eye perspective by spreading the lawn as a scenic backdrop, and in such a setting he painted his sister Andrée dandling her newborn son on her knee. But what energetic wit prevailed in his revision of this portrait and its transformation into an image as casual as a family snapshot, including the profile of the artist, who was the little boy's proud uncle.

Pierre Bonnard.
Family Scene, 1893.
Color lithograph,
12¼ × 7 in.
(31.2 × 17.7 cm).
Rogers Fund, 1922
(22.82.1–3)

Pierre Bonnard. *The Little Laundress,* 1896. Color lithograph, 11⅜ × 7¾ in. (29.4 × 20 cm). Harris Brisbane Dick Fund, 1939 (39.102.3)

Pierre Bonnard. *The Little Laundress,* 1896. Drawing in lithographic crayon, 12¼ × 8¼ in. (31.2 × 21 cm). The Elisha Whittelsey Collection, The Elisha Whittelsey Fund, 1988 (1988.1016)

Such a sight as this encounter between two Parisian waifs was common in Bonnard's day, when women and girls traversed the city to collect and deliver the daily wash. By the mid-1800s the laundry industry employed approximately one-fourth of the population of Paris and its environs. Laundresses gave drama to Zola's novel *L'Assommoir* (1877) and were featured in works by Daumier, Degas, and Henri de Toulouse-Lautrec. No one before Bonnard, however, had transformed a laundry girl into a simple, witty silhouette. Inspired by ukiyo-e woodcuts and probably by the comic figures of Hokusai, the artist surveyed the Parisian scene with all the zest of a Japanese master.

Three drawings, two in French private collections and one in the Metropolitan Museum (left), survive to demonstrate how precisely Bonnard planned his composition. In the earliest preparatory design, a floppy-eared mutt trots along the bottom of the page; in the intermediate drawing illustrated here, laundry girl and stray dog meet head-on in the street; in the latest version, the closest to the lithograph (opposite), the pedestrians seen crowding the top of the picture disappear, leaving girl and dog alone as kindred spirits, neither of whom apparently rates the use of the sidewalk.

Bonnard's *The Little Laundress* was one of twenty-two prints that the dealer Ambroise Vollard commissioned and published in a portfolio entitled *Album des peintres-graveurs.* The edition, limited to 100 impressions, was intended to involve painters actively in printmaking and to entice collectors. But even after Vollard displayed the prints in his gallery on the rue Laffitte and had Bonnard design a poster to advertise the show, the series was little noticed and sales were slow. The print collectors of the day were accustomed to more realistically described scenes and reluctant to accept the Impressionists' subject matter presented in the stringent shapes and charged palette of the Nabis.

Bonnard
96

On the occasion of his first one-man exhibition at the Galeries Durand-Ruel in 1896, Bonnard was praised in the pages of *La Vie artistique* (January 8), where the critic Gustave Geffroy observed, "No one can suggest more subtly the street scene, passing silhouettes, a colorful spot seen through a thin Paris mist." Bonnard was by this time gaining a reputation as a master chronicler of his city's incidental life, especially as it was played out in backstreets and busy thoroughfares. Although he soon complained of being stereotyped as an artist of urban scenery and after 1900 spent less and less time in the city, preferring to capture the light that fell on pastures and open-air verandas, he always returned to Paris, as if to make certain that the throb of activity persisted there and that he could still make poetic use of it.

When Bonnard created this color lithograph and eleven others in the suite entitled *Quelques Aspects de la vie de Paris,* his subject—the city—offered a fuller and more animated spectacle than had ever before been seen by a Frenchman. A burgeoning population crowded the boulevards and spilled from omnibuses onto the quays beside the Seine. The attractiveness of the city's broad avenues and the fashionable array of pedestrians had already been celebrated by Monet, Renoir, Caillebotte, Degas, Pissarro, and others, but Bonnard made of these sights something quite different. His concentrated vision shied away from identifying landmarks, favoring instead only the vaguest descriptions, so that pavements and railings, greatcoats and hansom cabs, became subsumed in bold abstractions expressing the city's patterns and rhythms.

Pierre Bonnard. *The Bridge.* From the suite *Quelques Aspects de la vie de Paris,* published in 1899. Color lithograph, 10⅜ × 16¼ in. (26.5 × 41.2 cm). Harris Brisbane Dick Fund, 1928 (28.50.4[9])

The rooms on the rue Saint-Honoré that Edouard Vuillard shared with his mother for nearly four decades served as her workplace as well as his. The painter often absorbed himself in the study of the papered walls and furnishings, while Mme Vuillard busied herself with the tasks of a professional corset maker.

The cloistered placidity of these interiors must have seemed to the artist at times soothing, at times stifling. His use of heavy colors, deep shadows, and sharp perspectives suggests a yearning for something beyond the embrace of the familiar ceilings and walls. The unsettled atmosphere differs significantly from the mood of seventeenth-century Dutch domestic pictures, with which Vuillard's work is often compared, where light funneled through windows and doors calmly defines the comforts of bourgeois life.

Vuillard's painting (right) may seem to continue the Dutch genre tradition by attentively describing the contents of a quiet room bathed in golden light. His lithograph (opposite), however, is a radical departure, compressing architectural space into a sheet of pulsating hues with a simple, planar scheme and colors of equal intensity for things both near and far.

Occasionally in his work, Vuillard reminds us that the rhythms of daily life, determined for so long by the rising and setting of the sun, were altered in the late nineteenth century by the use of oil, gas, and, around 1900, by electric light. The beribboned hanging lamp (perhaps adorned in celebration of its recent installation), undoubtedly prolonged daytime activities into the night, when life became centered around its illumination.

Edouard Vuillard, 1868–1940. *Interior with Figure,* 1896. Oil on panel, 19½ × 20¾ in. (49.5 × 52.7 cm). Robert Lehman Collection, 1975 (1975.1.225)

Edouard Vuillard. *Interior with a Hanging Lamp.* From a suite of twelve lithographs published in 1899. Color lithograph, 14 × 11⅛ in. (35.7 × 28.4 cm). Harris Brisbane Dick Fund, 1925 (25.70.23)

Edouard Vuillard. *The Avenue.* From a suite of twelve lithographs published in 1899. Color lithograph, 12⅛ × 16¼ in. (31 × 41.2 cm). Harris Brisbane Dick Fund, 1925 (25.70.18)

It is a pity that none of the stage sets Vuillard designed for plays by Ibsen and Strindberg at the Paris Théâtre de l'Oeuvre has survived. We can only imagine the decorative effect of these large backdrops prepared in the early 1890s. Close to them in period and scale are the eight-foot panels for residential interiors that Vuillard painted between 1892 and 1898 in distemper (the traditional medium of set production). Much smaller but nonetheless aspiring to room-size grandeur are certain of the color lithographs Vuillard printed in the late 1890s, like *The Avenue,* which are as broad and decorative as theatrical scenery and seem to leave open the possibility that they may be upstaged by live drama.

The series of nine panels depicting Parisian parks and gardens that Vuillard painted in 1894 for the dining room of Alexandre Natanson's apartment on the avenue du Bois de Boulogne (now the avenue Foch) can be compared to *The Avenue,* which also dwells on expanses of gravel and pavement strewn with figures and mottled by afternoon light. A restrained palette binds the elements of the scene, while rhythmic patterns are underscored throughout: in a woman's cape, in cracks in the street, and in alternating patches of sunshine and shade. The perspectival description of deep space is willfully contradicted so that a blaze of green at a point presumed distant projects itself toward the foreground. Thus, the line of curbstones, edging what is probably the expansive and fashionable avenue du Bois de Boulogne, leads the eye not to the verdant park at the promenade's end but rather to the top of the page. During his brief but fervent subscription to the theories of the Nabis group, Vuillard asserted both the preeminence of a picture's surface and the artist's right to subordinate his subject to formal concerns.

TISSERIE

Edouard Vuillard. *The Café at Night.* From a suite of twelve lithographs published in 1899. Color lithograph, 14⅛ × 10⅞ in. (35.4 × 27.6 cm). Harris Brisbane Dick Fund, 1925 (25.70.24)

By the late 1890s Parisians were able to sit down at nearly twenty-seven thousand cafés, most of which had cropped up along the new boulevards constructed by Baron Haussmann as part of his urban-renewal program during the mid-nineteenth century. The interiors and exteriors of cafés appear in late nineteenth-century pictures by Manet, Degas, Bonnard, Toulouse-Lautrec, and Seurat. It is to be regretted that Vuillard so seldom treated the subject, which was the public equivalent of the private sitting- and dining rooms he portrayed with such sensitivity. There was probably more activity and flux to café life than he cared to recall pictorially. He produced a number of small paintings on this theme, but the subject appears only once among his prints, in the album of twelve color lithographs that Vollard published early in 1899 at a high point in the artist's career.

When this print was created, electric lamps were well on their way to supplanting oil and gas lights in public places. Vuillard seems to have marveled at the transformed appearance of his city at night, its open-air rooms magically redecorated with sparkling glass and tabletops gleaming at the borders of darkness.

It is likely that Vuillard saw van Gogh's painting of a café in Arles at night (right), which was owned by the art critic Albert Aurier and exhibited in 1891 at the gallery Le Barc de Boutteville, where Vuillard, too, displayed his works. However, Vuillard, in contrast to van Gogh, was given to emphasizing, with a certain detachment, the diverting charms of a situation rather than dwelling upon its visceral impact. In that respect Vuillard leads us toward the decorations of Matisse and the planar designs (sometimes incorporating words and letters) of the Cubists Picasso and Braque.

Vincent van Gogh, 1853–1890. *The Café at Night, Place du Forum, Arles,* September 1888. Oil on canvas, 27⅝ × 35 in. (70 × 89 cm). State Museum Kröller-Müller, Otterlo, The Netherlands

Paul Signac, 1863–1935. *The Bell Tower at Saint-Tropez,* ca. 1896. Etching and aquatint, third (final) state, 8½ × 5¼ in. (21.5 × 13.5 cm). Museum of Fine Arts, Boston

Paul Signac. *The Port at Saint-Tropez,* 1897–98. Color lithograph, proof impression, 17⅛ × 13 in. (44 × 33 cm). The Elisha Whittelsey Collection, The Elisha Whittelsey Fund, 1987 (1987.1087)

A year after Gauguin set sail for Tahiti, Paul Signac embarked for Saint-Tropez. The death of Signac's best friend Seurat the previous year, in 1891, had been a blow, and he sought solace in his passion for sailing. The painter Henri-Edmond Cross's colorful descriptions of the South of France convinced Signac to sail his five-ton cutter *Olympia* down the Atlantic coast to the Midi Canal and into the Mediterranean Sea, where he discovered a small fishing village set on the shore of a gulf.

Saint-Tropez, which at that time could be reached easily only by sea, had recently been described by Guy de Maupassant in *Sur l'eau* (1888): "This isolated little port is one of the charming and simple daughters of the sea, one of those modest little towns, jutting into the water like a shell, nourished by fish and sea air. . . . You can see, on the paving of the streets, like pearls, the scales of sardines."

From the spring of 1892 until the onset of World War I, Signac spent the major part of every year in Saint-Tropez, attracting to his side many painters of his generation, Bonnard and Matisse among them. In 1897 he purchased La Hune, a house situated close to the beach and seaside activity. He frequently stationed himself at the port on the edge of the jetty, there to draw the stuccoed walls and canvas sails shimmering against the bright water.

As the principal spokesman of the Neo-Impressionists, Signac continued to be the driving spirit of the group after Seurat's death, for he remained convinced of the benefits of applying the laws of optics to art. At a time when modern science was coming of age, he

was persuaded that art required a scientific approach. The color theories of Eugène Chevreul (1839) and Charles Henry (1888, 1891) presented rationales for precise and methodical painting procedures opposed to the charming disorder of Impressionism. Signac applied these theories in a style he called Divisionism, stating: "To divide is to ensure all the benefits of luminosity, color, and harmony by the optical intermingling of pure colors." More important than simply painting in dots was the division of colors into their purer elements so that the eye could combine them for the most optically vibrant effect.

By about 1896, when Signac was given the assignment to produce the color lithograph illustrated here (which was intended for Vollard's third, but never completed, *Album des peintres-graveurs*), he had begun to relax his adherence to the strictest doctrines of the Neo-Impressionist school. With some detachment he began to interpret the ideas that had stirred him and Seurat a decade before, producing his major study, *D'Eugène Delacroix au Néo-Impressionnisme*, in 1899.

Signac's lithograph seems to reflect the artist's high spirits at this time, while affirming such guiding principles of Neo-Impressionism as Henry's theory that pleasure is associated with an upward direction and with movement from left to right. This print marks one of the many occasions on which the artist paired tall masts and sails with lofty towers. Structures rising majestically above land and sea often figured in the work of Signac (whose mother had wanted him to be an architect), beginning with his youthful painting of the scaffolding of Sacré-Coeur and continuing in views of Mont Saint-Michel, the domed churches of Venice and Constantinople, and the Houses of Parliament.

By 1896 Signac was no longer working directly in front of his subject but rather from drawings and notes in his studio. His increasing interest in the classical tradition brought a new clarity to the construction of his pictures, which he refined through repetition. An etching of the Saint-Tropez port (left), made about the same time as the lithograph, displays greater realistic detail, which Signac suppressed in the color print to serene and harmonious effect.

Henri de Toulouse-Lautrec, 1864–1901.
The Englishman at the Moulin Rouge, 1892. Oil and gouache on cardboard, 33¾ × 26 in. (85.7 × 66 cm). Bequest of Miss Adelaide Milton de Groot (1876–1967), 1967 (67.187.108)

The Moulin Rouge, which opened on the boulevard Clichy in 1889, offered bars, drinking gardens, music, and boisterous entertainment to a clientele mixed of the chic and the seedy, the well-mannered and the gross. Toulouse-Lautrec made his first color print, a five-foot poster, to revive attendance at the nightspot and a year later was commissioned by Boussod and Valadon to produce for collectors a pair of prints that featured the famous Moulin Rouge and a few of its regulars. Among them was the English painter William Tom Warrener, who, like Lautrec, was an aristocrat-turned-bohemian, slumming in Montmartre and thrilled to be part of the scenery, but an outsider all the same.

Lautrec immortalized his friend Warrener as the top-hatted gentleman who is seen vividly blushing at the risqué remarks of two flirts. The girls' lips are discreetly concealed behind a gigot sleeve, but Warrener's reddened ear (which appears in Lautrec's preliminary oil sketch at right) gives the clue to his discomfort. An encounter such as this was doubtless routine in the dance hall's atmosphere of tawdry commercialism, but Lautrec's rendition of the age-old theme is bold and incisive, thoroughly modern, and unforgettable.

A comparison of Lautrec's preliminary painting with his subsequent print (opposite) reveals just how completely he comprehended the special virtues of color lithography and how thoroughly he exploited them. The conversion from painterly realism to decorative abstraction was achieved through extraordinary discipline, ingenuity, and the strong influence of Japanese wood-block prints.

As complex as the process of color lithography is, Lautrec obviously found the technique enthralling and sometimes went to the trouble of working his ideas in oil paint before proceeding to five, six, or even seven color-printing stones. After discovering color lithography to be both the artistic argot of his time and an avenue to recognition, Lautrec dedicated himself to this process for almost a decade, producing, on the average, one lithograph every week to ten days.

Opposite
Henri de Toulouse-Lautrec. *The Englishman at the Moulin Rouge,* 1892. Color lithograph, second (final) state, 18⁹⁄₁₆ × 14⅝ in. (47.7 × 37.2 cm). Bequest of Scofield Thayer, 1982 (1984.1203.139)

T-Lautrec
Imp. Edw. Ancourt à Paris.

Henri de Toulouse-Lautrec. *The Loge with the Gilt Mask,* 1893. Color lithograph, 14⅝ × 11½ in. (37.3 × 30.4 cm). Bequest of Clifford A. Furst, 1958 (58.621.3)

Henri de Toulouse-Lautrec. *Cecy Loftus,* 1895. Color lithograph, 9¹³⁄₁₆ × 14½ in. (36.8 × 24.8 cm). Purchase, Derald H. and Janet Ruttenberg Gift, 1985 (1985.1015)

Nothing stirred Lautrec to artistic activity with greater effect than an entertainer's performance. Solo singers, dancers, and dramatic actors all were magnets to his imagination. He fixed on their distorted expressions sharpened by makeup and their quirky gestures enlarged by footlights. The artificial, exaggerated life of the stage seemed to provide a refuge for Lautrec, whom real life had treated cruelly, assigning him the bizarre role of the dwarfed, alcoholic son of old French aristocracy.

Practically all of Lautrec's lithographs were done for magazines, newspapers, book or sheet-music publishers, or for cabarets or theaters, such as the Théâtre Libre, which commissioned the program cover design illustrated on this page. Performers themselves called upon Lautrec to create advertising or souvenirs for their admirers, although sometimes the results were not entirely to their liking. "For heaven's sake, don't make me so horribly ugly. A little less, please . . . ," the chanteuse Yvette Guilbert once pleaded with Lautrec when she saw one of his portraits.

Lautrec's analysis of a performer, like that of the Scottish mimic Cecy Loftus (opposite), usually began with rapid sketches that he made while seated in the audience. The charged atmosphere of the theater and the dynamics of the performance were captured in crayon scrawls and spattered ink. Such wily images as the two shown here, with their Daumier-like nimbleness and their elastic expressions, are in themselves performances, as compelling and convincing as the stage artists' own.

Henri de Toulouse-Lautrec. *Chilpéric*, 1896. Oil on canvas, 57⅛ × 59 in. (145 × 150 cm). Collection of Mrs. John Hay Whitney, New York

Henri de Toulouse-Lautrec. *Mademoiselle Marcelle Lender*, 1895. Color lithograph, fourth (final) state Image: 12⅞ × 9½ in. (32.8 × 24.2 cm). Alfred Stieglitz Collection, 1949 (49.55.163)

Although Toulouse-Lautrec's infatuation with Marcelle Lender was less productive artistically than his attachment to either Jane Avril or Yvette Guilbert, the actress was the subject of no fewer than thirteen lithographs, ten drawings, and two paintings between 1893 and 1898. Dancing, singing, and bowing, Mlle Lender was treated full-face, in profile, and from the back, most often in the costume of Galswinthe, the Merovingian heroine in the 1895 staging of Hervé's outlandish operetta, *Chilpéric*.

Lautrec, who always preferred light musicals to serious drama, must have begun painting his stage-side view of Lender dancing the bolero in the revival of *Chilpéric* (right) about the time he executed a group of lithographs on the same theme. The most lavish of these prints, an eight-color production, was distributed in more than a thousand impressions with the Berlin magazine *Pan* during the first year of its publication. The brilliant evocation of theatrical glamor in this print—which simulates the splendor of both Merovingian enamels and Japanese woodcuts—nonetheless was denounced by the management of *Pan*. Its editor and art critic, Julius Meier-Graefe, was lambasted for publishing a "decadent," "poisonous" print, and the incident ultimately led to his dismissal.

Produced at the time when moviemaking was born (the first public film showing in Paris occurred in 1895), Lautrec's works are uncanny predictions of Hollywood's style of star promotion. For example, compared to the painting of Marcelle Lender's onstage performance

(above)—itself like a film still—his vivid close-up of her profile (opposite) has all the force of a publicity shot deliberately designed for wide distribution. Lautrec himself never lost sight of the fact that the artistic medium that brought him fame was identified with advertising, and he was never more effective than when he mixed his acerbic wit with lithographic ink.

Sources and Further Reading

Boggs, Jean Sutherland, Henri Loyrette, Michael Pantazzi, and Gary Tinterow. *Degas.* Paris: Galeries nationales du Grand Palais, Ottawa: National Gallery of Canada, New York: The Metropolitan Museum of Art, 1988.

Bouvet, Francis. *Bonnard: The Complete Graphic Work.* New York, 1981.

Boyle-Turner, Caroline (Foreword by Douglas Druick). *The Prints of the Pont-Aven School: Gauguin and His Circle in Brittany.* New York, 1986.

Brettell, Richard, Françoise Cachin, Barbara Stern Shapiro, et al. *Pissarro.* London: Hayward Gallery, Paris: Galeries nationales du Grand Palais, Boston: Museum of Fine Arts, 1981.

Brettell, Richard, Françoise Cachin, Claire Frèches-Thory, and Charles F. Stuckey, with assistance from Peter Zegers. *The Art of Paul Gauguin.* Washington, D.C.: National Gallery of Art, Chicago: The Art Institute of Chicago, 1988.

Cachin, Françoise. *Paul Signac.* Greenwich, Connecticut, 1971.

Cachin, Françoise, Charles S. Moffett, and Michel Melot (entries on Manet's prints by Juliet Wilson Bareau). *Manet 1832-1883.* Paris: Galeries nationales du Grand Palais, New York: The Metropolitan Museum of Art, 1983.

Carey, Frances, and Antony Griffiths. *From Manet to Toulouse-Lautrec: French Lithographs 1860-1900.* London: British Museum, 1978.

Castleman, Riva, and Wolfgang Wittrock, eds. *Henri de Toulouse-Lautrec: Images of the 1890s.* New York: The Museum of Modern Art, 1985.

Cate, Phillip Dennis, and Sinclair Hamilton Hitchings. *The Color Revolution: Color Lithography in France 1890-1900.* New Brunswick, New Jersey: Rutgers University Art Gallery, 1978.

Druick, Douglas, and Michel Hoog. *Fantin-Latour.* Ottawa: National Gallery of Canada, 1983.

Druick, Douglas, and Peter Zegers. *La Pierre Parle: Lithography in France 1848-1900* (text panels and labels for the exhibition). Ottawa: National Gallery of Canada, 1981.

Fisher, Jay McKean. *The Prints of Edouard Manet.* Washington, D.C.: International Exhibitions Foundation, 1985.

Ives, Colta Feller. *The Great Wave.* New York: The Metropolitan Museum of Art, 1974.

Janis, Eugenia Parry. *Degas Monotypes: Essay, Catalogue and Checklist.* Cambridge: Fogg Art Museum, Harvard University, 1968.

Kornfeld, E. W., and P. A. Wick. *Catalogue raisonné de l'oeuvre gravé et lithographié de Paul Signac.* Bern, 1974.

McMullen, Roy. *Degas: His Life, Times, and Work.* Boston, 1984.

Mellerio, André. *Odilon Redon.* Paris, 1913.

Mongan, Elizabeth, Eberhard W. Kornfeld, and Howard Joachim. *Paul Gauguin: Catalogue raisonné of his Prints.* Bern, 1988.

Moore, George. "Degas: The Painter of Modern Life," *The Magazine of Art,* 13 (1890), p. 425.

Redon, Odilon. *To Myself: Notes on Life, Art, and Artists.* Trans. Mira Jacob and Jeanne L. Wasserman. New York, 1986.

Reed, Sue Welsh, and Barbara Stern Shapiro (with an essay by Douglas Druick and Peter Zegers). *Edgar Degas: The Painter as Printmaker.* Boston: Museum of Fine Arts, 1984.

Reff, Theodore. *Degas: The Artist's Mind.* New York, 1976.

Reff, Theodore. *Manet and Modern Paris.* Washington, D.C.: National Gallery of Art, 1982.

Rewald, John. *The History of Impressionism.* 1st ed. 1946; 4th rev. ed. New York: The Museum of Modern Art, 1973.

Rewald, John. *Post-Impressionism from van Gogh to Gauguin.* 1st ed. 1956; 3rd ed. New York: The Museum of Modern Art, 1978.

Roger-Marx, Claude. *L'Oeuvre Gravé de Vuillard.* Monte Carlo, 1948.

Russell, John. *Edouard Vuillard 1868-1940.* Toronto: Art Gallery of Ontario, 1971.

Terrasse, Antoine. *Pierre Bonnard.* Paris, 1967.

Weber, Eugen. *France, Fin de Siècle.* Cambridge: Harvard University Press, 1986.

Wittrock, Wolfgang. *Toulouse-Lautrec: The Complete Prints.* 2 vols. London, 1985.

Zeldin, Theodore. *France 1848-1945: Intellect and Pride.* 1st ed. 1977; rpt. Oxford, 1980.

Notes

Introduction
Page 4, col. 1, li. 1: Zeldin, p. 41. Page 4, col. [illegible] li. 17: Weber, p. 27. Page 4, col. 1, li. 38: Drui[illegible] in Boyle-Turner, p. 11. Page 4, col. 3, li. 5: Druick in *Fantin-Latour,* p. 279. Page 4, col. 3, li. 51: McMullen, p. 358. Page 5, col. 1, li. 19: Carey, pp. 14-18. Page 7, col. 1, li. 12: Letter from Gauguin to Emile Bernard, November 1888, quoted in Rewald, *Post-Impressionism . . . ,* p. 180.

Page 12, li. 12: Letter from Fantin-Latour to Scholderer, 30 June 1879, quoted in Druick, *Fantin-Latour,* p. 257. Page 19, li. 9: Moore, p. 425. Page 20, li. 27: Moore, pp. 425-26. Pag[illegible] 24, li. 30, 37: Redon, pp. 103, 23. Page 26, col [illegible] 1, li. 37: Redon, p. 22. Page 28, col. 1, li. 20, 3[illegible] Letter from Gauguin to Schuffenecker, end of February or early March 1888, quoted in Rewald[illegible] *Post-Impressionism . . . ,* p. 171; see also Claire Frèches-Thory in Brettell, et al., *The Art of Paul Gauguin,* p. 95. Page 30, li. 8: Quoted in Rewal[illegible] *Post-Impressionism . . . ,* p. 487. Page 32, li. 1: "No[illegible] Noa," Louvre ms. 109-110 as quoted in Brettell, [illegible] al., *The Art of Paul Gauguin,* p. 280. Page 36, li. 6: Quoted in Bouvet, p. 8. Page 48, col. 1, li. 14[illegible] Quoted in Cachin, *Paul Signac,* pp. 56 and 22.

Inside back cover: Henri de Toulouse-Lautrec. *The Seated Clowness* (Mlle Cha-u-ka-o), 1896. Color lithograph, 20¾ × 15¾ in. (52.8 × 40.3 cm). Bequest of Scofield Thayer, 1982 (1984.1203.166[3])